REAL
mvpkids®

We're More Alike Than Different™

Sophia Day®

Written by Megan Johnson   Illustrated by Stephanie Strouse

The Sophia Day® Creative Team-

Megan Johnson, Stephanie Strouse, Marla Conn,
Kayla Pearson, Timothy Zowada, Carol Sauder, Mel Sauder

A **special thank you** to our team of reviewers who graciously
give us feedback, edits and help ensure that our products
remain accurate, applicable and genuinely diverse.

Published and Distributed by MVP Kids Media, LLC -
Mesa, Arizona, USA
Printed by RR Donnelley Asia Printing Solutions, Ltd -
Dongguan City, Guangdong Province, China

Designed by Stephanie Strouse

ISBN 978-164370761-7
DOM May 2019,
Job # 11-002-01

May your childhood be filled with adventure, your days with hope and your learnings with wisdom, and may you continuously grow as an MVP Kid, preparing to lead a responsible, meaningful life.

— SOPHIA DAY

I have a lot of friends

who are different than me.

We don't do things all the same,

and that's how it's meant to be.

But we're more alike than different.

Come along and you will see!

Can you name
some things you
like to do with
your friends?

Making new friends at the playground,

try to say "hello."

We may not understand each other.

We can play ball though!

Do you know someone who speaks a different language?

I'm sharing dinner with a friend.

It's sweet and sour pork.

"I eat it with my chopsticks."

"I eat it with my fork."

What kinds of ethnic foods do you like to eat?

When I meet someone different,

I don't need to be afraid.

I'll try to keep an open mind

and see new things their way.

We're more alike than different.

We'll just find new ways to play!

Why is it important
to celebrate
differences in
people?

We both like to make our music

and give our moms a show.

"I listen to it with my ears."

"I feel it head to toe!"

What musical
instrument do
you enjoy?

Playing freeze tag on the playground,

we run, skip, hop and jog.

"I join them with my speedy wheels.

That's how I move along."

What do you like to play when you are on the playground?

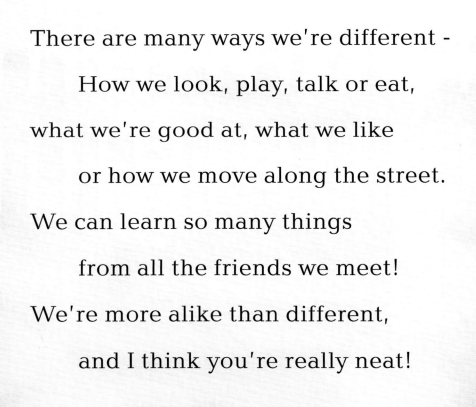

There are many ways we're different -

How we look, play, talk or eat,

what we're good at, what we like

or how we move along the street.

We can learn so many things

from all the friends we meet!

We're more alike than different,

and I think you're really neat!

What have you
learned from
a friend?

City or country, wherever we live,

we have fun when we're together.

We'll ride a horse or the city train

in any kind of weather!

Where do
you live?
City, suburbs
or country?

The two of us look much the same;

we're brother-sister twins.

Adoption made us brothers, too,
with different colored skin!

How are you alike
and different from
your siblings?

Sometimes we see someone so different

that it's hard to understand

how they do things, how they learn,

or how to be their friend.

What are ways that you can love others?

It's okay to look,

    but please don't point or stare.

Let's celebrate our differences

    instead of being scared.

Use kind words, ask questions

    and you'll make friends everywhere!

What are some examples of kind words that you can use when you meet people who are different from you?

We're more alike than different,

and here's one way we're the same:

everybody needs a friend.

So come on, friend, let's play!

How are you
and your
friends alike?

meet our

mvpkids®

featured in
We're More Alike Than Different™

Annie James

Blake James

Julia Rojas

Miriam Nasser

Yong Chen

Liam Johnson

Olivia Wagner

Aanya Patel

Frankie Russo

Leo Russo

Gabby Gonzalez

Lucas Miller

LeBron Miller

Sarah Goldstein

Faith Jordan

Ezekiel Jordan

HELPFUL TEACHING TIPS
Head. Heart. Hand.

Informing Minds

It is good and natural for children to develop a sense of pride in their family and heritage. It is possible to nurture both your child's self-pride and respect for the differences of others. Real MVP Kids® aims to help your child build both confidence and compassionate awareness by providing relatable characters with a variety of backgrounds, ethnicities, religions, abilities and special needs with whom your child can identify.

Children's brains are wired to make sense of patterns and puzzles and to fit new experiences into categories of things they've previously known. Because of this it is natural for children to point out differences and ask questions. There is nothing wrong with observing and talking about differences in people. Sometimes these conversations should take place privately with your child. Other times it may be appropriate to ask questions in attempt to make a new friend. In fact, parents of children with special needs often say they would rather talk and answer respectful questions than have their child pointed out, stared at or ignored. It is our job as parents and caregivers to nurture this observing into appreciating and celebrating rather than fearing and rejecting.

Certain differences such as body type or mental health issues may be taboo to discuss in public. These topics change periodically according to cultural shifts. If your child makes a comment about a subject that might be taboo, diffuse the situation with a statement such as, "There are a lot of ways that people are different. Please don't be rude." Then address the topic privately with your child. Remember to share with your child that there could be many different reasons for what they observe. Be careful not to make character judgments based on first impressions or observed differences.

The words we use in observing differences are important. Words that pass judgment can often be replaced by words that make an observation. These exact phrases may change over time, but the heart of the matter stays the same: use words that are kind and respectful. Also, our attitudes and reactions are more important than the exact words we use. You may find these phrases helpful if your child accidentally says something hurtful in public. If you are parenting a child with visible differences, these phrases might be helpful in gently correcting others.

Judgment	Observation
"What's wrong with...?"	"What's different about...?"
(not) normal	(not) typical
weird, freaky, ugly	unusual, unique, different
retarded, crazy, stupid	thinks differently, brain works differently
fat, thin, short, other body description	built differently

There are some special needs and differences that the average person describes without meaning to pass judgment. People from these backgrounds might not be offended, but may prefer a subtly different way of describing their situation. Preferred language will change depending on the specific difference, but below are a few examples to illustrate why certain terms are preferred. Making an effort to learn the accepted language of a particular subculture shows compassion. In many cases you can ask someone, "How do you prefer to describe..."

Common	Preferred
is special needs/ special needs child	has special needs/ child with special needs
is autistic/ autistic child*	has autism/ a child with autism*
(Down Syndrome, etc.)	*(Down Syndrome, etc.)*
is adopted	was adopted
real family/parent	birth family/ parent
	(step and adoptive parents and families are real)

Some parents don't mind, or even prefer, to describe their child with his or her diagnosis first as a way to celebrate how that diagnosis makes their child special. When you get to know someone, you can ask which they prefer.

Exposing your child to the concept of celebrating differences will help develop a worldview that respects and appreciates diversity. The wider a child's worldview the more compassionate and accepting your child will be, rather than self-centered and judgmental.

Remember that most children ask questions out of genuine interest or concern. Be gentle in your responses to children's curiosity and model kindness. Especially if a comment is directed toward you or your child, gently correct a child rather than scolding them so that you do not damage their willingness to build relationships with people who are different than them.

Children often do not notice a difference in skin colors. When they do begin to notice, we can work to battle racism with simple responses such as, "Yes, her skin is darker/lighter than yours. It is really beautiful." As our children grow, it is important to expose them to literature and other media that shows different ethnic backgrounds in equally positive light.

When your child negatively points out a difference in someone else, find a way to spin it into something positive, perhaps using the chart on the previous page to find an appropriate word. Next, help your child see at least one way that person is similar to them, such as, they have a nice smile or like to play in the sand. This will help your child build empathy and look past a first impression.

It is natural for people to build their strongest relationships with others who are very similar. Parents and caregivers set the example for how their children interact with people who are different. Take a look at your own circles of friends, coworkers and neighbors. Are you making an effort to have friendships with others of different backgrounds, race, religion and abilities?

*For additional tip and reference information, visit **www.mvpkids.com**.*

If you know ahead of time that your child is going to encounter someone with a specific difference, prepare them for the meeting. Describe how the person is different and what they can expect from the encounter, then explain how they should behave. (For example, "Great-grandma is much older than we are and she doesn't hear well. Use a strong voice to talk to her and don't feel hurt if she doesn't respond." or "Leo uses a walker because he needs extra help to move around. When we meet him at the park today, let's play on the concrete so his wheels can turn easily.")

Teach your child to adjust their tone of voice when asking questions so as not to convey that something is wrong with or about whom they are speaking. If you prefer, teach your child not to mention differences in public, but to ask you questions privately.

If your child does say something inappropriate or offensive to a stranger in public, a simple apology is more helpful than shushing your child and hurrying them away from the person. Hurrying away would only affirm your child's statement. It may be uncomfortable to approach the person, but doing so teaches your child that this person should not be feared or ostracized.

Take your child to a busy public park and observe people from a distance. Give your child a visual scavenger hunt. For example, find 1) a child wearing blue, green or pink, 2) a person using a walker, cane or wheelchair, 3) people with different shades of skin, 4) someone wearing a hat, headscarf or other head covering, 5) the oldest person and youngest person at the park. Help your child find descriptive words that are appropriate. Next, help your child find people who are similar, teaching that people can be both similar and different.

Yellow flowers are a traditional symbol of friendship, compassion and respect. Help your child look for and count the yellow flowers on each page of *We're More Alike Than Different™*.

Directing
Hands

Grow up with our mvpkids®

Our **CELEBRATE!**™ board books for toddlers and preschoolers focus on social, emotional, educational and physical needs. Helpful Teaching Tips are included in each book to equip parents to guide their children deeper into the subject of each book.

Our **Help Me Become**™ series for early elementary readers tells three short stories of our MVP Kids® inspiring character growth. Each story concludes with a discussion guide to help the child process the story and apply the concepts.

Our **Help Me Understand**™ series for elementary readers shares the stories of our MVP Kids® learning to understand and manage a specific emotion. Readers will gain tools to take responsibility for their own emotions and develop healthy relationships.

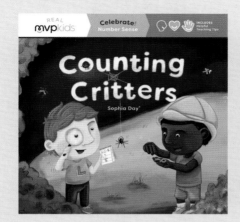
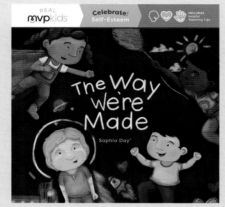
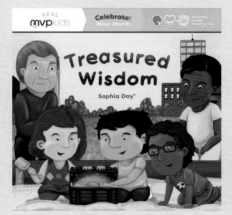
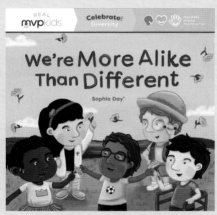
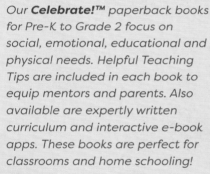

Yong Chen

Leo Russo

Frankie Russo

Julia Rojas

Aanya Patel

Faith James

Blake James

Sarah Goldstein